Series / Number 04-011

Toward a Theory of
Issue Voting

C. ANTHONY BROH
State University of New York at Geneseo

SAGE PUBLICATIONS / Beverly Hills / London

For information address:

SAGE PUBLICATIONS, INC.
275 South Beverly Drive
Beverly Hills, California 90212

SAGE PUBLICATIONS LTD
St George's House / 44 Hatton Garden
London EC1N 8ER

International Standard Book Number 0-8039-0358-8

Library of Congress Catalog Card No. 73-92213

FIRST PRINTING

CONTENTS

Toward a Theory of

Issue Voting

C. ANTHONY BROH
State University of New York at Geneseo

This paper will attempt to specify several conditions under which issue voting is likely to take place. In doing so, it moves toward a "theory" of issue voting by explaining contradictory positions about the importance of issues in the voting decision. The hypotheses and variables are drawn from previous research which has disputed the existence of an issue aware public rather than specified the conditions for issue voting.

Much of the voting behavior literature can be categorized by one of the following three hypotheses:

(A) People vote according to their issue attitudes.

(B) Issue voting is dependent upon level of conceptualization of politics.

(C) Issue voting is dependent upon the perception of party difference on issues.

Let us look at some of the major studies which can illustrate each of these hypotheses.

AUTHOR'S NOTE: *This study began as a Ph.D. dissertation at the University of Wisconsin at Madison. I wish to thank Charles F. Cnudde, Jack Dennis, and Murray Edelman whose suggestions and comments were an indispensable aid to the completion of this project. The data utilized in this paper were made available by the Inter-university Consortium for Political Research. The data were originally collected by the Survey Research Center Political Behavior Program and were given to me by*

REVIEW OF THE LITERATURE

PEOPLE VOTE ACCORDING TO THEIR ISSUE ATTITUDES

This hypothesis was best supported by the late V. O. Key, Jr. in *The Responsible Electorate* (1966). Key's methodology was to divide the electorate into three major voting patterns. First, "standpatters" were those who voted for candidates in the same party for two successive elections. Secondly, the "switchers" were those who voted for candidates of the opposite party for two successive elections. Thirdly, the "new voters" were those who were either too young or did not happen to vote in the first of two elections.

Key then showed the relationship of the six voting patterns to issue attitudes collected by the American Institute of Public Opinion from 1936 to 1960.[1] The data consistently showed a pattern of policy concern and issue voting among the segments of the population. Switchers were likely to have changed parties because of their policy agreement or disagreement with members of the governing party. New voters voted for their issue position and standpatters voted for the same party that favored their issue position (Key, 1966: 149-151). Key concluded that "all these patterns of behavior are consistent with the supposition that voters, or at least a large number of them, are moved by their perceptions and appraisals of policy and performance" (Key, 1966: 150).

ISSUE VOTING IS DEPENDENT UPON
LEVEL OF CONCEPTUALIZATION

Key's data was probably not intended to show the rational electorate as some would have it, but clearly it was intended to demonstrate that "voters are not fools" and that partisan choice in some elections some of the time is related to policy alternatives (Campbell, 1966: 1008). Much of the work growing out of the Survey Research Center is a specification of this discussion. If Key's intention was to show a relationship between issues and voting, the SRC has attempted to specify who does issue voting. *The American Voter* and Converse's work on "belief systems" are exemplary (Campbell, et al., 1960; Converse, 1964).

the Data and Program Library Service of the University of Wisconsin. Computer time was awarded by the Graduate Studies Committee of the University of Wisconsin. I also wish to thank the Political Science Department of the State University of New York at Geneseo for providing funds to type the final draft of this manuscript. Finally, my thanks to John S. Jackson who read an earlier draft of this paper and to Patti James who typed, edited, and proofed the final version. The aforementioned are, of course, absolved of any responsibility for the contents of this paper.

Like Key, Campbell, et al. looked at defection rates over two successive elections. In 1956 defection was least likely at the highest level of conceptualization: that is, persons who switched were least likely to conceptualize politics in "ideological terms" (Campbell, et al., 1960: 264). Since they also showed that the most partisan were also the most involved, the best educated, the most issue oriented (Campbell, et al., 1960: 188-215), it follows that issue voting took place only at the highest levels of conceptualization.

What the SRC meant by levels of conceptualization was clarified by Converse in his discussion of "belief systems" (Converse, 1964). Converse used four different measures of conceptualization which conformed to the several definitions of ideology found in the voting literature.[2]

With each measure, mass publics were shown to have little constraint, organization, or consistency in their conceptualization of politics. Converse's conclusions are quoted below:

> A realistic picture of political belief systems in mass public is not one that omits issues and policy demands completely nor one that presumes widespread ideological coherence; it is rather one that captures the fragmentation, narrowness, and diversity of these demands (Converse, 1964: 247).

This "fragmentation, narrowness, and diversity" is generally given the interpretation that few people, in fact, have a high level of conceptualization of politics. Furthermore only those who do have high conceptualization might be expected to vote according to issue and policy positions.

At least two articles question the small number of ideologues in the electorate. John Field and Ronald Anderson argued that "the number of people making ideological evaluations of the parties and presidential candidates does vary from one election to another and that, at least in 1964, this change had something to do with the stimuli of the campaign" (Field and Anderson, 1969). A second study by John Pierce came to much the same conclusion. He found that Converse's conclusions underestimated the proportion of "conceptual ideologues" in the 1964 election (Pierce, 1970).

Both of these latter studies are suggestive of an important addition to the previous literature. The idea that the number of ideologues changes over time introduces campaign, environmental factors into the discussion of conceptualization of politics. Though both the Field-Anderson and the Pierce articles suggest the presence of such an influence, neither attempts to measure it.

In sum, at least three common elements run through the "belief system" literature. First Campbell, et al., Converse, Field-Anderson, and Pierce all view conceptualization of politics as a dimension which explains issue orientation to voting. In the operational sense, level of conceptualization of politics is a variable to be measured and to describe issue attitudes in making a voting decision. Second, level of conceptualization of politics is a long-run indicator which measures the political sophistication an individual has developed over a period of years. Field-Anderson and Pierce suggest the probable influence of campaign factors but neither introduces variables that might measure its added influence on issue voting. Third, the literature is impressive in its attempt to measure ideological thinking (high conceptualization of politics) in several ways. The foundation for this work has been laid by Converse; others cite his monograph for an explanation and definition of terms.

ISSUE VOTING IS DEPENDENT UPON PERCEPTION OF PARTY DIFFERENCE ON ISSUES

Recent literature in voting behavior has placed greater emphasis on campaign variables. Increasingly researchers have noticed an ability of the electorate to differentiate the two parties on key issues that have been emphasized during the campaign. While these conclusions do not negate the earlier discussion of low conceptualization of politics, they do introduce a new and important variable to the maze of voting studies.

Perception of party difference is the recognition of issue stands of the political parties during a given campaign. One might expect that increased party contact, increased exposure to mass media, and increased campaign interest would tend to clarify the issue stands of the two parties during a campaign—especially if the two parties can be easily differentiated. This ability might be related to a long term level of conceptualization of politics, but it is by no means the same thing. Perception of party difference is a short term campaign indicator of political sophistication. In short "accurate perception" may be due to media bombardment or to contact by a precinct captain or to the differences in the issues developed by the particular candidates in a given campaign. It may in no way reflect a general or long term sophistication of political thinking.

Several studies have tended to emphasize campaign perception of party difference. The first was a multi-dimensional scale technique employed by Herbert Weisberg and Jerrold Rusk (1970). They analyzed thermometer scores of affect toward the 1968 candidates, party, and several social welfare issues. They found a "party dimension" and an orthogonal "issue dimension" which discriminated between Wallace and LeMay at one end and McCarthy and Kennedy at the other. Furthermore, social welfare and economic issues that realigned the parties during the depression loaded highly on the party factor. This dimension space of issues and party explaining candidate affect is, of course, a short term view of party difference and issue difference.

A second article which emphasized perception of party difference on issues was presented by David RePass (1971). He was interested in the most "salient" issues and the party preference of the voter for each "issue concern." He found that the greater the number of salient issues perceived by the individual, the more likely the voter was to perceive a single party as being best able to handle the problems; furthermore, a voter was more likely to follow his party position on several salient issues than he was to follow his party identification. RePass's conclusions are worth stating in toto:

> What is important to observe from this study is that by and large the voting public has at least a few substantive issues in mind at the time of an election, and the voters seem to be acting more responsibly than had previously been thought.... When we allow voters to define their own issue space, they are able to sort out the differences between parties with a fair degree of accuracy. It would probably be going too far to say that the public has contextual knowledge upon which to base its decision. But we have shown that the public is in large measure concerned about specific issues, and that these cognitions have a considerable impact on electoral choice (RePass, 1971: 400).

Third, Gerald Pomper has argued that accurate perception of party differences on issues has increased from 1956 to 1968. For six issues the public showed greater perception of party difference regardless of party identification, age, education, region, or race. Pomper concluded that this more "perceptive electorate now more fully satisfies one of the basic conditions for a responsible party system" (1971; 1972).

Finally Benjamin Page and Richard Brody have argued that perception of the party nominees on the Vietnam War issue was quite accurate in 1968 (Page and Brody, 1972). Indeed the ambiguity of the campaign stimulus was reflected in a failure to see a difference in candidates and general confusion on the issue.

In sum these three articles represent the current trend in voting behavior research. Weisberg-Rusk, RePass, Pomper and Page-Brody have all placed heavier emphasis upon the perception of issues during the campaign than upon long term conceptualization on an ideological continuum. A major shortcoming has been the view that increased accurate perception refutes the earlier work on conceptualization of politics. Though perception of party difference is an additional variable to be considered, it is not the only variable that explains voting behavior. Advances in the voting behavior literature can best be made by realizing the independent effects of issue attitudes, conceptualization of politics, and perception of party difference on issues.

THE RESEARCH DESIGN

THE HYPOTHESES

I have presented three variables that are said to be an influence on voting: issue attitudes, long term conceptualization of politics, and perception of party difference on issues. From the review of the literature and from the description of the several factors influencing voting, it is now possible to state some hypothesized relationships between these variables. The first model simply states that voting is a function of issue attitudes:

$$V = k_1 x_1$$

Where V is voting, k_1 is a constant, x_1 is issue attitudes.

This, of course, is the model of voting suggested by V. O. Key originally.

The second model is an interaction model. It states that issue attitudes are not very important in the voting decision except for persons with higher levels of conceptualization of politics. This model can be represented as follows:

$$V = k_1 x_1 \cdot k_2 x_2$$

Where k_2 is a constant, x_2 is level of conceptualization of politics, and all other symbols are the same as above.

This is the model implied by the writing emanating from the Survey Research Center and elaborated upon by Converse in his discussion of "belief systems."

Finally the introduction of campaign perception of party difference on issues as a specifying variable for the above relationship suggests a third interaction model. It states that issue voting takes place at higher levels of conceptualization of politics, but this depends also upon a campaign in which the voters differentiated the parties according to specific issues. This more elaborate campaign-communication model can be described by the following interaction model:

$$V = k_1 x_1 \cdot k_2 x_2 \cdot k_3 x_3$$

Where k_3 is a constant, x_3 is perception of party difference on issues, and all other symbols are the same as above.

Should the data fit this final model this research will have moved in the direction of reconciling many of the inconsistencies and contradictions in the voting literature. Whereas the previous literature emphasized the lack of issue voting, the present study seeks to specify the conditions under which it takes place. It thereby seeks to explain the presence and absence of such behavior in the United States.[3]

THE VARIABLES

Candidate Preference. The candidate preference of the respondent was determined by asking who he (she) voted for for President. If the person did not vote, he was asked who he would have voted for if he had voted.[4] My coding makes two departures from the SRC. First I combined voters and non-voters into one category for each candidate. Second, persons who refused to state for whom they were voting, persons who voted for a third party, persons who could not remember or stated no preference, and persons who could not be located for a post-election interview were combined into an "other" category.[5]

Voters and non-voters were combined to include the entire electorate in the research. In the discussion of social-psychological models, it is important to include the entire sample. Presumably such models concern human characteristics and should extend to non-voters and voters alike. In this sense, my discussion is not tied to actual voting behavior, but it goes beyond some voting discussions which attempt to explain only partisanship or party identification.

Issue Attitudes. Nine policy questions were selected to measure the issue attitudes of voters in the election. The issues were the power of the federal government, medical aid, federal ownership of public utilities, the Civil Rights Act of 1964, job discrimination, public school desegregation, federal aid to education, job guarantees, and prayer in public schools. These issues affected almost every segment of the population and were the major components of the 1964 campaign.[6]

With each question it is possible to view a "greater federal role" dimension. Each question was coded into three categories: (1) Greater federal role (2) Neutral including "don't know," other, refused, etc. (3) Lesser federal role. These categories provide an ordinal dimension of issue attitudes which can then be correlated with other ordinal indices.

Conceptualization of Politics. The operational definition of conceptualization of politics is consistent with previous research. A person with high conceptualization has the ability to separate partisan choice on a consistent issue dimension.

Respondents were asked if there was anything in particular they liked or disliked about the two political parties.[7] This question produced four categories of answers: positive statements about Democrats, negative statements about Democrats, positive statements about Republicans, and negative statements about Republicans. Of course not all statements referred to political issues. Using previous measures of conceptualization as a guide, only the statements which related to issues were extracted. A scale was then developed which represents issue responses to the likes and dislikes of the two political parties. Each like and dislike was coded -1 or $+1$ depending on the partisanship of the statement. With a maximum of 5 responses in each category this scale ranges from -10 to $+10$ and represents issue responses to the parties.[8] Persons who could consistently name several issues in a partisan direction presumably showed a greater level of conceptualization of partisan politics than either persons who were not consistent in their issue responses or who could only name fewer issues.[9]

Perception of Party Difference on Issues. In this analysis perception has been dichotomized. Respondents were asked which political party was more likely to want the government to increase its role in several issue areas. In each case it was apparent from historical discussion that the Democratic Party at the national level was more likely to take the position: It is rather clear that the Presidential candidates, themselves, were divided on the issues.[10] Persons who recognized the position of the Democratic Party in the 1964 election were recorded as having an "accurate" perception; others, including don't know, seeing no difference, and a Republican Party response were "mis-perceivers."[11]

In sum, three testable models are prevalent in the voting behavior literature. The first states that voting is a function of issue attitudes. The second states that voting is a joint function of issue attitudes and levels of conceptualization of politics. The third states that voting is a joint function of issue attitudes, levels of conceptualization of politics, and perception of party difference on issues.

Each of these models is a specification of the previous model and can be tested by controlling for an additional variable. One might test for interaction by investigating the multiplicative values of the cells in a contingency table.

Finally each of the three specifying variables has been operationally defined. By physical controls it is possible to introduce new variables to the model. Increasing correlations are empirical evidence of an interaction effect which makes specification possible. It is now possible to test each of the voting behavior models.

MODEL ONE:
THE ISSUES AND CANDIDATE PREFERENCE

The first stage of this analysis requires a close look at the relationship of opinions about domestic issues in the 1964 campaign to voting behavior. Nine issues have been selected for this purpose: power of the federal government, medical aid, federal ownership of public utilities, the Civil Rights Act of 1964, job discrimination, public school desegregation, federal aid to education, job guarantees, and prayer in public schools.

One of the major issues of the 1964 campaign was a complicated one that struck at the major theme of the Goldwater strategy. Republicans traditionally have attacked the "dominating and "entangling" bureaucracy in Washington, but Barry Goldwater's denouncements were so vehement that this issue became a major theme of his campaign (White, 1965: 316). The problem was tailor-made for the Senator who had a long record of opposition to farm subsidies, Rural Electrification, TVA, National Labor Relations Board, and even the Supreme Court (White, 1965: 317). In describing the issue Goldwater wrote:

There are a number of ways in which the power of government can be measured. . . . [One] is the extent of government interference in the daily lives of individuals. The farmer is told how much wheat he can grow. The wage earner is at the mercy of national union leaders whose great power is a direct consequence of federal labor legislation. The businessman is hampered by a maze of government regulations and often by direct government competition. The government takes six per cent of most payrolls in Social Security Taxes and thus compels millions of individuals to postpone until later years the enjoyment of wealth they might otherwise enjoy today. Increasingly the federal government sets standards of education, health, and safety [Goldwater, 1960: 20-21].

If Goldwater was clear on his statement of the problem of big government, he was equally clear on his position in the matter.

I have little interest in streamlining government or in making it more efficient, for I mean to reduce its size. I do not undertake to promote welfare, for I propose to extend freedom. My aim is not to pass laws, but repeal them. It is not to inaugurate new programs, but to cancel old ones [Goldwater, 1960: 23].

Lyndon Johnson was, of course, equally clear on the issue. As the incumbent President he ran on his record; and it was a record of new programs, new legislation, increased welfare benefits, etc. which he termed "The Great Society." Johnson made no apologies for the federal government and proclaimed his programs showed "vision" and "faith" in the future (Kessel, 1968: 240). Recalling the 1964 campaign, Lyndon Johnson has written:

> The program we submitted to the voters during the 1964 campaign would commit the nation to press on with the War on Poverty, to provide greater educational opportunities for all American children, to offer medical care to the elderly, to conserve our water and air and natural resources, and to tackle the country's long-standing housing shortage [Johnson, 1971: 104].

From these statements it would appear that the two candidates had opposing views about the role of government and that each was on record with his position. With such clear differentiation, it is not surprising to find that candidate preference among the electorate was related to attitudes toward the power of the federal government.[12] The data are presented in Table 1. Eighty-one percent of those who felt the government had not gotten too strong showed a preference for Lyndon Johnson, while a majority (57%) of those who felt the government was getting too powerful favored Barry Goldwater.

In some ways the medical aid issue was the "opposite side of the same coin." The Johnson strategy was to pick a particular program that was popular and campaign for increased benefits. This would force Goldwater to take an unpopular position. Thus Johnson proposed health and medical care for the elderly as an added benefit to the social security program.[13]

Goldwater's official position on medicare was somewhat different than his campaign position. Officially he stated he favored a sound social security system and he wanted to see it strengthened. But the headlines shaped his position more than his statements. In Concord, New Hampshire, Goldwater suggested that one way to improve social security might be to make it voluntary. Since it would be impossible to offer medical aid or social security benefits to the elderly without mandatory participation by young workers, the reaction of the press could have been expected. The headline of the Concord *Monitor* the next day left little ambiguity: GOLDWATER SETS GOALS: END SOCIAL SECURITY (White, 1965: 317-318). Presumably medicare would go with it.

As might be expected, opinions of the electorate on medicare were related to candidate preference.[14] Three out of four persons who felt the federal government should get involved in medical aid favored

Johnson; 56% of those opposed favored Goldwater, as noted in Table 2.

The third issue of the campaign is similar to medical aid in that Barry Goldwater's position was exaggerated due largely to his campaign strategy. In order to prove his ideological consistency in offering a "choice" to the voters, Goldwater often chose potentially hostile audiences to announce major policy positions. He had campaigned against medicare in Florida, against the "War on Poverty" in West Virginia, and then chose Nashville, Tennessee to urge the abolition of Rural Electrification and the selling of the Tennessee Valley Authority.

The effect of this strategy was to differentiate very clearly the candidates on the issue of government ownership of public utilities. By saying very little on the subject, the incumbent President was in an obvious position of favoring government ownership of power plants; Goldwater had raised the issue in such a way that it made his position equally clear. Candidate preference of the electorate as it related to this issue is presented in Table 3.[15] The data show that 86% of those who felt government should own power plants favored Lyndon Johnson while only 53% of those who felt electric power should be left to private business favored Johnson.

With the backdrop of voter registration drives in rural areas of the South, riots in the central city of several large urban areas, and the candidacy of George Wallace, civil rights was a major concern of many voters. Theodore White, the self-appointed historian for the elections of the 1960's, reported that both candidates "jointly decided to exclude from the campaign dialogue as far as possible any appeal to racism" (White, 1965: 319).[16]

Even without much campaign rhetoric, the records of the two candidates seemed rather clear. Goldwater took a break in his campaign to return to Washington and vote against the Civil Rights Act of 1964. The action was against the recommendations of his advisors, for it portrayed the Senator as an anti-Negro candidate. But there is not much question that Goldwater had voted against the Act out of conviction. His position on school desegregation had been outlined in *The Conscience of a Conservative:*

> The federal Constitution does *not* require the States to maintain racially mixed schools. Despite the recent holding of the Supreme Court, I am firmly convinced—not only that integrated schools are not required—but that the Constitution does not permit any interference whatsoever by the federal government in the field of education [Goldwater, 1960: 35].

TABLE 1. THE RELATIONSHIP OF OPINIONS ON THE POWER OF THE FEDERAL GOVERNMENT TO CANDIDATE PREFERENCE

	Candidate preference[a]			
	Johnson	Other[b]	Goldwater	Total
The government has not gotten too strong	81%	8%	11%	100%[d] (562)
Neutral[c]	70	13	17	100 (536)
The government is getting too powerful	33	10	57	100 (473)

[a]Candidate Preference is described above.

[b]"Other" includes DK, NA, other, refused, no post-interview.

[c]"Neutral" includes other, DK, NA, no interest.

[d]Numbers in parentheses are the total number of respondents in each category.

[16]

TABLE 2. THE RELATIONSHIP OF OPINIONS ON MEDICARE TO CANDIDATE PREFERENCE

	Candidate preference			
	Johnson	Other	Goldwater	Total
Help people get doctors and hospital care at low cost	77%	11%	13%	101[a] (778)
Neutral	65	13	22	100 (355)
Government should stay out of this	37	8	56	101 (438)

[a]Numbers do not total 100 due to rounding.

[17]

TABLE 3. THE RELATIONSHIP OF OPINIONS ON GOVERNMENT OWNERSHIP OF
ELECTRIC POWER PLANTS TO CANDIDATE PREFERENCE

| | Candidate preference | | | |
	Johnson	Other	Goldwater	Total
Government should own power plants	86%	2%	13%	101% (280)
Neutral	62	20	18	100 (723)
Leave this to private business	53	2	45	100 (586)

It was not until the closing days of the campaign that Senator Goldwater delivered a major speech on the issue. Speaking at a $100-a-plate dinner in Arizona, he opposed the busing or otherwise mixing of school children for the purpose of compulsory desegregation. To integrate schools with fixed proportions of races, nationalities, or religions, according to the Arizonan, was "morally wrong and offensive to freedom" (Kessel, 1968: 210).[17]

The relationship of candidate preference to three civil rights issues are presented below. The Civil Rights Act of 1964 specifically dealt with public accommodations; its relationship to candidate may be found in Table 4.[18] Job discrimination and school desegregation also showed a relationship to candidate preference, as shown in Tables 5 and 6. In each of these tables it can be seen that persons favoring a pro-civil rights position were more likely to prefer Johnson than persons who felt the government should stay out of civil rights enforcement.

The issue of federal aid to education strikes deep at the hearts of most conservatives. Barry Goldwater was no exception. "Some Notes on Education" outlined very clearly the objections of the Senator to the federal aid to education program:

Let us . . . note four reasons why federal aid to education is objectionable.
The first is that federal intervention in education is unconstitutional.
The second objection is that the alleged need for federal funds has never been convincingly demonstrated.
The third objection to federal aid is that it promotes the idea that federal school money is "free" money, and thus gives the people a distorted picture of the cost of education.
The fourth objection is that federal aid to education inevitably means federal control of education [Goldwater, 1960: 79-83].

Lyndon Johnson's position on federal aid to education also seemed clear. On October 12 in Denver, Colorado, the President pledged to make educational opportunities available to all:

I intend to put education at the top of America's agenda. And if you do not quite understand the details of what I mean by the top of America's agenda, I will say this: That regardless of family status education should be open to every boy and girl born in America up to the highest level which he or she is able to master [Kessel, 1968: 244].

It can only be assumed that Johnson was serious with these goals. Less than a year after his re-election, he signed the Aid to Education Act and

TABLE 4. THE RELATIONSHIP OF OPINIONS ON THE CIVIL RIGHTS ACT OF 1964 TO CANDIDATE PREFERENCE

	Candidate preference			
	Johnson	Other	Goldwater	Total
Government should support the right of Negroes to go to any hotel or restaurant	81%	2%	17%	100% (671)
Neutral	47	39	14	100 (348)
Government should stay out of this	50	3	47	100 (552)

[20]

TABLE 5. THE RELATIONSHIP OF OPINIONS ON GOVERNMENT GUARANTEE OF FAIR EMPLOYMENT FOR NEGROES AND CANDIDATE PREFERENCE

	Candidate preference			
	Johnson	Other	Goldwater	Total
Government should see that Negroes get fair treatment in jobs	76%	9%	16%	101% (611)
Neutral	62	13	25	100 (334)
Leave those matters to state/local government	51	11	39	101 (626)

99291 [21]

TABLE 6. THE RELATIONSHIP OF OPINIONS ON SCHOOL INTEGRATION AND
CANDIDATE PREFERENCE

	Candidate preference			
	Johnson	Other	Goldwater	Total
Government should see to it that white and Negro children go to the same school	73%	8%	20%	101% (647)
Neutral	63	15	22	100 (322)
Government should stay out of this	52	11	37	100 (602)

boldly proclaimed that "no act [meant] more to the future of America" (Johnson, 1971: 212).

These statements help clarify the position of the two candidates on this issue. Since it appears that they were diametrically opposed on federal aid to education, it is not surprising that there is a relationship between the opinions of the electorate on this issue and candidate preference.[19] The results are presented in Table 7. Seventy-six percent of those favoring federal aid to education preferred Johnson while only 51% of those opposed favored Johnson. On the other hand, 40% of the opponents to federal aid favored Goldwater while only 15% of the proponents favored Goldwater.

The eighth issue, guaranteed employment for all Americans, was part of the program Johnson referred to as "quality of life." Under the slogan "Hire—Train—Retain," Lyndon Johnson was able to persuade the National Alliance of Businessmen to launch a program to hire the "hard-core unemployed in the ghettos and slums of America's fifty largest cities" (Johnson, 1971: 332). Though it may be debatable whether this 1965 program was as effective as Johnson's description in his memoirs, there is little doubt that the goal of a guaranteed job was consistent with other proposed "Great Society" programs during the 1964 campaign. As described earlier the President made no apologies for new programs and government innovations to increase the so-called "quality of life." Rather it was Barry Goldwater's attack on big government and massive bureaucracy that made "guaranteed employment" an important issue of the campaign. The relationship of opinions on the issue to candidate preference is presented in Table 8.[20]

The last issue in the analysis was chosen because neither candidate expressed a position openly during the campaign. However, their attitude on prayer in public schools might be inferred by looking at the groups to which they appealed. One scholar has reported that the greatest national reaction to *Reynolds v. Sims* was the proposal on constitutional amendments (Wasby, 1970: 129). Of the 100 Congressmen introducing amendments most were Republicans or Southern rural Democrats, two of the major groups in the Goldwater coalition.[21] While it is not altogether clear that Johnson opposed prayer in public schools (there is no mention of the subject in his memoirs), one might assume that such a position would be consistent with liberals and the religious minorities in the Democratic coalition. On the other hand, Johnson's southern background and fundamentalist religious training might suggest he would have opposed the Reynolds decision. At best the positions of the two candidates were unclear and the relationship of the public's opinions with candidate

TABLE 7. THE RELATIONSHIP OF OPINIONS ON FEDERAL AID TO EDUCATION AND CANDIDATE PREFERENCE

| | Candidate preference | | | |
	Johnson	Other	Goldwater	Total
Schools should get help from federal government	76%	10%	15%	101% (490)
Neutral	69	14	18	101 (355)
Should handle education at state or local level	51	9	40	100 (726)

TABLE 8. THE RELATIONSHIP OF OPINIONS ON A GUARANTEED JOB TO CANDIDATE
PREFERENCE

	Candidate preference			
	Johnson	Other	Goldwater	Total
Should see to it that every person has a job	76%	9%	16%	101% (611)
Neutral	62	13	25	100 (334)
Should let each person get ahead on his own	51	11	39	101 (626)

preference reflects this confusion. Table 9 shows that there was a relatively small relationship between the two.[22]

For all three categories of opinion, the percentage preferring Johnson was about the same (62%–68%); and for all three categoties the percentage preferring Goldwater was about the same (23%–28%). One of the most interesting points of this table is the overwhelming number of people who favored prayer in the public schools. Of the 1571 responding, 1,169 or 74% were expressing opposition to the Supreme Court ruling. These data suggest that Goldwater might have missed an opportunity to take a "conservative" position that was extremely popular with the electorate.

SUMMARY

The nine domestic issue attitudes described above give a summary of public opinion on domestic policy during the 1964 Presidential campaign. They are issues that touched almost every segment of society. Unlike most campaigns, the strategies of each candidate provided the voters with clear alternatives on major policy positions that were to be decided by government in the years ahead. Lyndon Johnson's memoirs describe this election from the "vantage point" of one candidate:

> Goldwater asked the voters to give him a mandate to abolish Social Security; I asked for a mandate to expand it with Medicare. Goldwater called for a return to a sink-or-swim policy toward the poor; I called for an expanded government program to eradicate poverty. Goldwater called for a strengthening of states' rights. I called for more federal protection for civil rights. Goldwater favored what amounted to an unregulated economy; I favored imaginative fiscal and monetary policies that could eliminate the old cycles of boom and bust [Johnson, 1971: 103].

In short, whatever else might be recorded about the 1964 election, the voters were offered alternatives on domestic issues. Clearly the Arizona Senator's goal to offer a "choice not an echo" was realized.[23]

Not only was a "choice" offered to the voters, but they responded to the alternatives with their candidate preference. Gamma coefficients between the opinions of the electorate on the nine issue areas and the candidate preference are shown in Table 10.[24] It can be observed that the candidate preference of the electorate showed a substantial correlation with every issue on which it was possible to ascertain the candidates' position. The school prayer issue showed only a .08 gamma coefficient; all other issues were at least .31 and extended to .60 for opinions on government power.

The theoretical implications of these findings cannot be overlooked. The year 1964 was chosen as a case study, in part, because the election was known to offer clear policy alternatives to the voters. By choosing this election it is possible to establish the maximum conditions in recent years to begin the search for the effect of issues. The correlations shown above are higher for this election than might be expected between issues and candidate preference in any other presidential year. These data, however, do suggest V. O. Key's observation, that an electorate is "moved by concern about central and relevant questions of public policy," has support in the 1964 election.

But evidence of a relationship between candidate preference and issue attitudes is not all that is involved in the controversies of the current voting literature. Specification of that relationship is also important. For example, the Survey Research Center would seem to argue that the relationship described above is due either to the "ideological" few in society who have a belief system that allows them to respond to issue orientations in a consistent manner or to the especially dramatic character of the campaign and candidates in the 1964 election itself.[25] We now turn to these questions.

MODEL TWO:
ISSUE VOTING AND CONCEPTUALIZATION

The second model of voting behavior states that issue voting is dependent upon level of conceptualization. Thus, the relationships presented earlier and predicted by the first model do not give a complete picture of voting behavior. The addition of a controlling variable can help specify the conditions under which Model One behavior takes place.

The writings emanating from the Survey Research Center have emphasized levels of conceptualization as a specifying variable for issue voting. A high level of conceptualization of politics has been defined as "ideological thought" of the structural, personal, organizational, and location type.[26] This is a more complex relationship than Model One.

It is possible to make several predictions about the correlations between issue attitudes and voting preference for different levels of conceptualization of politics. The correlations should be monotonic and increasing as one goes up the ladder of increasingly higher levels of conceptualization. The model predicts the correlations should be increasing because of the interaction that takes place between issue attitudes and conceptualization.[27] The correlation coefficient itself measures the degree to which

TABLE 9. THE RELATIONSHIP OF OPINIONS ON PRAYER IN PUBLIC SCHOOLS TO CANDIDATE PREFERENCE

	Candidate preference			
	Johnson	Other	Goldwater	Total
Religion does not be-long in school	68%	9%	23%	100 (234)
Neutral	63	14	24	101 (168)
Should start school each day with a prayer	62	10	28	100 (1169)

TABLE 10. CORRELATION OF ISSUES WITH CANDIDATE PREFERENCE

Government power	.60
Medicare	.54
Equal public accommodations	.45
Electric power plants	.41
Job guarantee	.41
Aid to education	.39
Equal job opportunity	.37
School desegregation	.31
Prayers in public schools	.08

issue attitudes vary with the dependent variable. If this correlation is higher for the high levels of conceptualization of politics and lower for the low levels of conceptualization of politics, the interaction of the two variables has been demonstrated. One might also expect monotonacity since more interaction would be expected to take place at higher levels of conceptualization.

It would be possible to predict the exact increases of the correlations between issue attitude and vote preference for conceptualization levels if there were no error factor. However, problems in measurement and outside influences make the exact ratio increases impossible to predict (Blalock, 1969: 156-162). The hypotheses for Model Two can be satisfied by simply showing a monotonic-increasing line tracing the correlation coefficients. However, approximately equal slopes add credibility to the reliability of the data and the theory.

The data for Model Two are presented in Figure 1. For eight of the nine domestic issues in the analysis, the correlation between issue attitudes and voting preferences increases at each level of conceptualization. For example, the correlation between attitudes on Medicare and voting preference increases from .36 at the lowest level of conceptualization to .59, then .65, and finally to .80 at the highest level of conceptualization. Government power, equal public accommodations, equal job opportunity, federal aid to education, and school desegregation also show an increasing relationship with vote preference at each level of conceptualization.

The issue of a job guarantee also shows a general trend for increasing correlations, but monotonacity is interrupted at the second level of conceptualization. The decrease from .31 to .28 is slight and might be accounted for by measurement error. However, this decrease at the second level of conceptualization occurs more frequently later and is worth noting. It may be that the ability to align one like or dislike with party positions is not as good a measure of conceptualization as the ability to make two, three, or more consistent alignments.[28] Nevertheless issue voting generally increases over the four levels of conceptualization for the guaranteed job issue.

Only one issue, prayers in public schools, does not show increasing correlations over the range of the conceptualization measure. As Figure 1 demonstrates, the prayers in public schools issue has a gamma correlation of .02 at the lowest level of conceptualization and −.01 at the highest level of conceptualization.[29] This, of course, is what one might expect since greater understanding of politics would not clarify issue positions that the candidates did not make. Neither Johnson nor Goldwater discussed prayer in public school; thus correlations that either increase or decrease must be

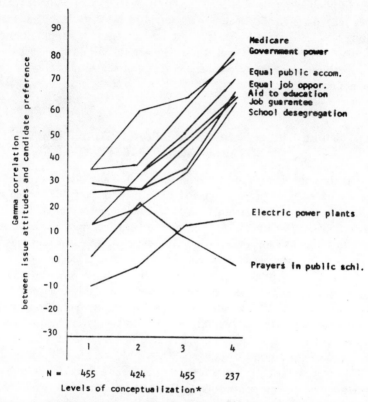

FIGURE 1. CORRELATION OF ISSUE ATTITUDES WITH CANDIDATE PREFERENCE
FOR LEVELS OF CONCEPTUALIZATION.

*Each level of conceptualization of politics reflects the number of
likes and dislikes that the respondent volunteered in an open-ended
question and that represented a consistent partisan direction.
Categories were collapsed as follows: level 1 was a net score of 0
partisanship; level 2 was a net score of -1 or +1; level 3 was -3, -2,
+2, +3; level 4 was less than -3 or greater than +3.

due to random error or systematic differences that do not show up for the
entire population.[30]

Finally it can be noticed that the slopes of the increasing correlations
for each issue attitude are approximately the same. If one could control all
outside influences on the indicators, one might expect perfectly parallel
lines. The tendency for all issues to have approximately the same slope
gives additional credibility to the analysis.

In sum the data presented here tend to confirm the model of voting behavior implicit in the works of the Survey Research Center. Issue voting does take place in the electorate as described by V. O. Key; but issue voting also increases at higher levels of conceptualization as suggested by Campbell, et al., Converse, and others. The latter model of voting behavior is a specification of the former. The evidence presented here confirms an earlier untested speculation.

MODEL THREE: ISSUE VOTING, CONCEPTUALIZATION, AND PERCEPTION OF PARTIES

The third model of voting behavior states that issue voting is dependent upon level of conceptualization and perception of party difference on issues. The relationship presented in the second model and implied by the Survey Research Center does not give a complete picture of voting behavior. The addition of a second controlling variable can help specify the conditions under which Model Two behavior takes place.

The test of this model can be made by observing issue voting at various levels of conceptualization of politics for both "misperceivers" and "accurate perceivers." The latter were people who were able to identify the Democratic Party as more likely to favor greater government action in each of the nine issue areas. Misperceivers were persons who could not make this identification.[31]

One expects the correlations for accurate perceivers to increase through higher levels of conceptualization. However, misperceivers would not appear to have sufficient information about the issues of the campaign to separate the two parties. Consequently one might expect the correlations to remain the same regardless of increased conceptualization of politics. Thus even the most sophisticated political thinkers must partake in campaign perceptions required for issue voting.

Figure 2 presents the data for the correlations between issue attitude and voting preference for "misperceivers." For all issue attitudes the correlations remain relatively constant across levels of conceptualization of politics.[32] For example, the correlation between Government Power and voting preference for misperceivers is .34 at the lowest level of conceptualization. There is a slight increase to .45 before the leveling off at .43 for the highest two levels of conceptualization of politics. School Desegregation and the Equal Public Accommodations issues both show similar results. Correlations at the lowest level of conceptualization of politics are .01 and .03, respectively, and at the highest are .06 for both issues. Other domestic economic issues show similar correlations.

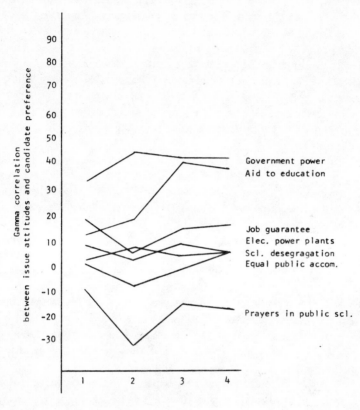

Level of conceptualization*

FIGURE 2.   CORRELATION OF ISSUE ATTITUDES WITH CANDIDATE PREFERENCE AT
            LEVELS OF CONCEPTUALIZATION OF POLITICS FOR MISPERCEIVERS.

*N for each correlation between issue attitudes and voting preference is
 as follows: Aid to education, 356, 273, 252, 108; Government power, 352,
 283, 274, 107; Medicare, 275, 202, 169, 60; Job guarantee, 322, 229, 213,
 93; School prayer, 394, 360, 394, 189; Equal job opportunity, 318, 233,
 202, 88; School desegregation, 327, 240, 212, 110; Electric power plants,
 373, 306, 295, 122; Equal public accommodations, 276, 217, 214, 91.

Also of importance are the relatively constant correlations through levels of conceptualization on the School Prayer issue. At the lowest level, the correlation is −.10; at the highest level it is .16. Without accurate perception persons are unable to make generalizations about how to vote, even if they have a fairly sophisticated level of conceptualization of politics. To the person trying to influence public policy with his vote, this would be an extremely frustrating situation.

Figure 3 presents the correlations between issue attitude and vote preference for "accurate perceivers."[33] These persons were able to identify correctly the Democratic Party as advocating a specific policy in the 1964 campaign. One would expect increased correlations between issue attitudes and voting preference for increasing levels of conceptualization of politics.

All nine domestic issues from the 1964 election have correlations with voting preference as expected. School Desegregation and voting preference, for example, have a gamma coefficient of .44 at the lowest level of conceptualization of politics for accurate perceivers. This increases to .53 at the second level, to .64 at the third level, and to .91 at the highest level of conceptualization of politics. The general attitude toward Government Power is also typical for accurate perceivers. The correlations increase from .67 at the lowest level of conceptualization to .97 at the highest level.

One of the most dramatic increases is between attitudes on School Prayer and voting preference for accurate perceivers. The gamma correlations increase from −1.00 at the lowest level of conceptualization of politics to .67 at the highest level. Since it is not clear exactly what each of the parties' positions on the issue actually was, accurate perception takes on a somewhat different meaning. It would appear that party positions were projected by this group of persons during the campaign even though the candidates themselves had not actually taken stands. Persons with high conceptualization of politics projected positions that would be consistent with civil liberties expectations of the parties; that is, the Democrats favor a separation of Church-State relations on the issue.[34] Persons with low conceptualization of politics projected the reverse relationship which accounts for the negative correlation.

It may also be noticed that most of the lines tracing the correlations of accurate perceivers are approximately parallel. That each of the issue attitudes behaves in similar fashion when various controls are introduced gives added reliability to the measurement of the variables and the theoretical framework developed in this research.

Also it can be observed from Figure 3 that persons at the highest level

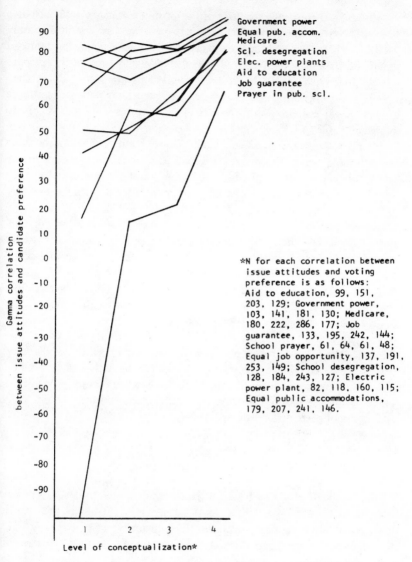

FIGURE 3. CORRELATION OF ISSUE ATTITUDES WITH CANDIDATE PREFERENCE AT LEVELS OF CONCEPTUALIZATION OF POLITICS FOR ACCURATE PERCEIVERS.

of conceptualization of politics who are accurate perceivers actually approach unity in correlating issue attitudes with voting preference. For example, the correlations for three of the most salient issues at the highest level of conceptualization for accurate perceivers are .97, .96, and .91.[35] These data conform to expectations since accurate perception would increase the ability of all persons to match issue attitudes and voting preference. That the gamma correlations approach 1.00 at the upper levels of conceptualization for accurate perceivers demonstrates that a very large percentage of the variance in voting behavior is being explained.[36]

Finally a comparison of accurate perceivers and the electorate as a whole is important to the analysis. Figure 4 demonstrates the general trend for accurate perceivers, misperceivers, and the entire electorate on the School Desegregation issue. At all four levels of conceptualization of politics the correlations with voting preference are higher for accurate perceivers than for the general electorate; for misperceivers the correlations are lower than the general electorate. Interaction has been demonstrated by this increase and decrease in correlations while physically controlling for a subset of the population.

In sum, the data presented here confirm the expectations suggested by the third model of voting behavior. Without exception the correlations between issue attitudes and voting preference for misperceivers remained constant regardless of increased level of conceptualization of politics. On the other hand, persons who perceived the campaign positions of the two parties accurately showed increasing correlations between issue attitudes and voting preference for increasing levels of conceptualization of politics. These findings confirm the interaction effect of conceptualization and perception of party difference on issue voting.

SUMMARY AND CONCLUSIONS

Three models of voting behavior have been presented. In Model I there was evidence to suggest that issue voting took place in the 1964 Presidential election. This conclusion was originally suggested by V. O. Key though his data and methods were different than those presented here.

Model II suggested that issue voting took place to a greater extent at higher levels of conceptualization of politics and to a lesser extent at lower levels of conceptualization of politics. This conclusion was originally suggested by writings emanating from the Survey Research Center. The

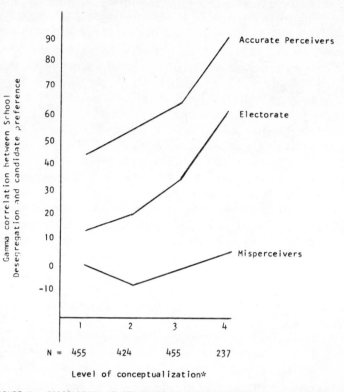

FIGURE 4. CORRELATION OF ATTITUDES ON SCHOOL DESEGREGATION WITH CANDIDATE PREFERENCE FOR THE ELECTORATE, MISPERCEIVERS, AND ACCURATE PERCEIVERS.

*N for each correlation between School Desegregation attitudes and voting preference for the four levels of conceptualization were: Accurate Perceivers, 128, 184, 243, 127; Electorate, 455, 424, 455, 237; Misperceivers, 327, 240, 212, 110.

data supporting this argument were consistent for nine issue attitudes in the 1964 campaign for four levels of conceptualization of politics.

Model III suggested that issue voting took place to a greater extent for increasing levels of conceptualization of politics only for persons who perceived a difference of the two parties on the issues. Misperceivers showed a constant correlation of issue attitudes and voting preference for all four levels of conceptualization of politics. These conclusions were consistent with recent research which has placed greater emphasis on the campaign for influencing voting preference.

Each of these models has been supported by data from the 1964

Presidential election, and each model is a more complex relationship than the previous model. What has often been presented as contradictory research by other scholars, has here been shown to be compatible models of behavior. Indeed Model Three is derived from Model Two and Model Two from Model One. Perception of party difference and levels of conceptualization of politics help specify the conditions of issue voting. The more complex models are an addition, not a contradiction to previous research.

In the quest for a "general theory" of social science, many scholars have suggested criteria for theoretical advancement. A theory is a statement about human behavior which is deductive, capable of being measured, parsimonious, predictive, and compatible with previous research (Meehan, 1967: 107-110; Blalock, 1969: 2-10; Kerlinger, 1964: 10-17). The models of issue voting presented in this research have moved in the direction of fulfilling these theoretical criteria.

Though some scholars have argued that formal theory requires deductive reasoning from a set of "universally accepted axioms," in the social sciences such propositions would probably not go far beyond the obvious.[37] Thus scholars are likely to settle for tentative theories of the middle range based on empirical tests of propositions held together by causal inference. Indeed the "verification" of such theories involves the rejection of competing alternatives rather than the acceptance of the theory itself (Blalock, 1969: 12).

Thus the introduction of new variables into a theoretical relationship has become an acceptable (if not the only) method of expanding social science theory (Blalock, 1969: 17-21). In the voting study presented here, the addition of new variables made explanation of a previous relationship possible. Issue voting in 1964 was found to take place under specific conditions: when there was a high level of conceptualization of politics and when there was a perceived difference of the two parties on campaign issues. The theoretical significance of the research presented here is in the specification of incomplete theories about issue voting into models made more complex only by the addition of single variables. Though such a test does not satisfy the purist demand for deduction, it does explain several causally linked variables with a single model.

Second, the theoretical concepts in the discussion are capable of being measured, making the theory testable. Voting preference, issue attitudes, levels of conceptualization of politics, and perception of party difference represent various aspects of voting and ideological thought. Each variable has had an operational indicator that is consistent with the concept it is said to represent.[38] Indeed many of the past contradictions on the subject of issue voting have been a result of insufficient operational definitions. The research presented here is a step toward clarification.

Third, a theory in the social sciences should involve parsimonious relationships stated in simplified terms. The research presented here has moved in this direction. Each of the three independent variables were concepts that are familiar to students of voting behavior; they are derived from recognized definitions of ideology that have persisted through the issue voting literature; and they have been stated with the precision of causal equations.

In one sense the non-additive model of interaction has made the issue voting model more complex. However, the contribution of this research was to include several previously studied variables into a single issue voting model. The interaction itself is a reflection of the way the influences on issue voting actually behave. The complexity of the methodology has in fact reduced several hypothesized relationships to a single model of issue voting behavior.

Mathematics provides the researcher with the most precise language for stating causal relationships.[39] Not only have the variables and correlations of this research been discussed verbally, but precise equations of specific voting models have been described mathematically. At this point in the theoretical development, it is not possible to describe all the terms of the equation with the precision of other sciences; that is measurement error and disturbing influences do exist. However, drawing these variables into an equation that is understood using conventional definitions of terms that have general usage and understanding in the discipline is a major step toward the elegance and precision required for more scientific advancement.

The fourth criteria for theoretical advancement is predictability. In no other area is the contribution of this research as clear. Throughout the discussion the emphasis has been on specifying the conditions of issue voting. The major thrust of the project has been to move the discussion from a conflict over the importance of issues to a realization of the conditions that create issue voting.

Prediction is involved at two levels. In one sense, the test of any hypothesis involves prediction since all possible outcomes of the observations must be anticipated in advance. After the "experiment" a decision is made whether or not to reject the hypothesis (Blalock, 1960: 91).

Prediction in the second and theoretical sense involves more than just hypothesis testing. A social science theory should be able to make predictions about future events. The application of research presented here is illustrative. In future elections one might predict that the voting decision is more likely to involve issue attitudes when the voter shows a relatively high degree of political sophistication and when the campaign presents relatively clear policy alternatives between the two political parties. Such a prediction is more theoretical than the previous state of affairs which simply disputed the importance of issue attitude.

A fifth criterion used to describe a theory is compatibility. A valid explanation should mesh, to a certain degree, with other research in the field and previous experience with the subject matter (Meehan, 1967: 107). Of course, a new theory is not totally compatible with the theory it is intended to replace or it would not replace it. However, the new theory must "explain away" or incorporate the old theory or it simply exists as contradictory evidence. In this sense a new theory explains more or draws out the conditions of the old theory.

Indeed the original impetus for this research was to move beyond an often misinterpreted conflict in the issue voting literature. Some scholars have viewed the voting literature as conflicting evidence on the importance of issues. According to this position, one group of scholars has argued that issues are relatively unimportant in the voting decision; another group has argued that issues are important. To the extent that such arguments are believed by leading scholars in a discipline, they represent a theory of issue voting.[40] Let us look at the proponents and opponents of the theory.

The discussion of the insignificance of issues has deep roots in the literature. In Bernard Berelson, et al., the electorate was presented as having little interest, motivation, knowledge, principle, or rationality in its voting decision (Berelson, Lazarsfeld, and McPhee, 1954: 307-311). In Angus Campbell, et al., the electorate was said to be influenced by party identification rather than ideological considerations (Campbell, et al., 1960: 188-265). In Philip Converse the electorate was said not to have an "integrated belief system" (Converse, 1964: 255). These studies from the voting literature plus other discussions in related fields represent a consistent presentation of the insignificance of issues at the mass level.[41]

Scholars of the opposite view have done much to perpetuate the argument on the importance of issues. V. O. Key's posthumous editors and critics, for example, probably overstated Key's intention to show voter rationality (Campbell, 1966: 1007). David RePass's opening sentence on issue saliency states that "leading studies of voting behavior have often concluded that specific issues are not a salient element in the electoral decision" (RePass, 1971: 389). Gerald Pomper begins "students of politics have frequently sneered at the inability of the 'masses' to discern political reality" (Pomper, 1972: 415). Indeed each of these scholars and others in related studies have presented counter-evidence to a theory proclaiming the unimportance of issues in the voting decision.

The research presented here has gone beyond this apparent conflict by presenting a broader theory which states the conditions necessary for issue voting. Much of the previous contradiction was perhaps tied to the era of politics in which the research was done. Issues were not raised as clearly by the two political parties during the 1950s (Kessel, 1972: 462). However, under circumstances in which there was a maximum amount of issue awareness, it has been possible to discover conditions which are likely to increase issue voting. Thus the special circumstances of the 1964 Presidential campaign have made possible the expansion of voting research toward a more general theory of issue voting.

On the other hand, the findings of this research are based upon a single election. The year 1964 was a special case in that it presented presidential alternatives like few other elections in the Twentieth Century. The data can only be interpreted with this in mind.

In conclusion there has been evidence from 1964 that the conditions for issue voting can be specified. Persons with higher levels of conceptualization of politics are more likely to be able to relate issue attitudes to voting preference than persons with lower levels of conceptualization. However, a basic recognition of the positions of the two political parties is necessary. That is, a higher level of conceptualization of politics is likely to produce issue voting only if there is an accurate perception of the issue difference between the two political parties.

Finally this research is far from the final statement in issue voting. It has not produced a theory of voting from which other propositions about voting behavior might be derived. However, by meeting several criteria for theoretical advancement, the models discussed in this study have moved in the direction of a theory of issue voting.

NOTES

1. The American Institute of Public Opinion, hereafter referred to as AIPO, is also known as the Gallup Poll.

2. The discussion of the operational definitions used by Converse is based on David W. Minar (1961).

3. The data in this research were originally collected by the Survey Research Center as one in a series of election studies conducted every two years since 1948. The probability sample in 1964 consists of 1571 persons of voting age living in private households in the continental United States. Respondents were selected in a manner which represents all strata of society for all regions of the country.

The Data and Program Library Service of the University of Wisconsin has made these data available through its membership in the Inter-University Consortium for Political Research. The original tapes, in many cases, were recoded and punched on cards to put them in a format for processing. All analyses were performed through the use of "software" made available at the Madison Academic Computing Center. Support for the research came from the National Science Foundation as a Project Assistant in the summer of 1971 and from the University of Wisconsin Graduate School Research Committee which awarded computer time for the project.

4. The actual wording was: "In talking to people about the election we find that a lot of people weren't able to vote because they weren't registered or they were sick or they just didn't have time. How about you, did you vote this time or did something keep you from voting? Who did you vote for for President? (No did not vote) Who would you have voted for for President if you had voted?"

5. Each respondent was interviewed twice, once before the election and once after the election. Pre-election interviews were conducted from September 7 to November 2; post-election interviews were conducted from November 20 to January 23. Only 121 of the 1571 persons in the sample could not be located for a post-election interview.

6. A detailed discussion of the assumptions and correlates of the variables in this section can be found in C. Anthony Broh (1972: 41-45).

7. The actual wording of the question was: "Is there anything in particular that you like about the Democratic (Republican) party?" "Is there anything in particular that you don't like about the Democratic (Republican) party?"

8. Actually this scale is one of the elements discussed by Angus Campbell, et al. (1960: 128-136), in their original field theory of party identification. The coding was done by the Survey Research Center.

9. For a detailed discussion of the assumptions in this index, see Broh (1972: 37-41).

10. For a detailed discussion of this point, see Broh (1972: 53-67).

11. Fromer and Skipper used a four-point scale of increasing misperception: Democrats, don't know, no difference, Republicans. Their data was for the 1960 election in which the positions of the Presidential candidates were not as clear. I have collapsed categories so as to have a greater number of persons in each cell.

The actual wording was: "Some people don't pay much attention to the political campaigns. How about you, would you say that you have been very much interested, somewhat interested, or not much interested in following the political campaigns so far this year?"

12. The actual wording of the question was: "Some people are afraid the government in Washington is getting too powerful for the good of the country and the individual person. Others feel that the government has not gotten too strong for the good of the country. Have you been interested enough in this to favor one side over the other? (If yes) What is your feeling, do you think: the government is getting too powerful or the government has not gotten too strong?"

13. That Johnson combined the Social Security and Medicare program into one issue can be seen by reading his memoirs. Writing of Goldwater's mistakes, he states: [Goldwater] "traveled to Florida, the retirement home of millions of Americans, and denegrated Medicare." (Johnson, 1971: 102). Actually it was Social Security. Or later, Johnson wrote, "I asked them [the voters] for a mandate to expand it [Social Security] with Medicare" (Johnson, 1971: 103).

14. The actual wording of the question was: "Some say the government in

Washington ought to help people get doctors and hospital care at low cost, others say the government should not get into this. Have you been interested enough in this to favor one side over the other? (If yes) What is your position? Should the government in Washington: help people get doctors and hospital care at low cost or stay out of this?"

15. The actual wording of the question was: "Some people think it's all right for the government to own power plants while others think the production of electricity should be left to private business. Have you been interested enough in this to favor one side over the other? (If yes) Which position is more like yours, having the: government own power plants or leaving this to private business?"

16. Kessel also notes that Goldwater made no direct appeals to racism. He points out that Goldwater sought a meeting on July 24, 1964 with Johnson to make such an agreement. Also Goldwater made the same promise to Republican leaders at a "Hershey unity conference" following the convention (Kessel, 1968: 109n).

17. This position, of course, laid the groundwork for George Wallace's American Independent Party in the 1968 election. "Busing to achieve racial balance" is once again a main issue of the 1972 campaign. In the Democratic Party George Wallace and Henry Jackson have openly opposed "busing." On the Republican side, President Nixon has moved to cut federal funds for busing and to intervene in court cases involving "forced busing." This issue would appear to be a major campaign theme which will divide Democrats and Republicans once again.

18. The actual wording of the three questions was:

"Congress passed a bill that says that Negroes should have the right to go to any restaurant they can afford, just like white people. Some people feel that this is something the government in Washington should support. Others feel that the government should stay out of the matter. Have you been interested enough in this to favor one side over the other? (If yes) Should the government: support the right of Negroes to go to any hotel or restaurant they can afford or stay out of this matter?"

"Some people feel that if Negroes are not getting fair treatment in jobs the government in Washington ought to see to it that they do. Others feel that this is not the Federal government's business. Have you had enough interest in this question to favor one side over the other? (If yes) How do you feel? Should the government in Washington: see to it that Negroes get fair treatment in jobs or leave these matters to the state and local communities?"

"Some people say that the government in Washington should see to it that white and Negro children are allowed to go to the same schools. Others claim that this is not the government's business. Have you been concerned enough about this question to favor one side over the other? (If yes) Do you think that the government in Washington should: see to it that white and Negro children go to the same schools or stay out of this area as it is none of its business?"

19. The actual wording on the aid to education question was: "Some people think the government in Washington should help towns and cities provide education for grade and high school children; others think that this should be handled by the states and local communities. Have you been interested enough in this to favor one side over the other? (If yes) Which are you in favor of: getting help from the government in Washington or handling it at the state and local level?"

20. The actual wording of the question was: "In general, some people feel that the government in Washington should see to it that every person has a job and a good standard of living. Others think the government should just let each person get ahead

on his own. Have you been interested enough in this to favor one side over the other? (If yes) Do you think that the government: should see to it that every person has a job and a good standard of living or should it let each person get ahead on his own?"

21. For a detailed study of the groups in the Goldwater coalition, see Kessel (1968: 182).

22. The actual wording of the question on prayer in public schools was: "Some people think it is all right for the public schools to start each day with a prayer. Others feel that religion does not belong in the public schools but should be taken care of by the family and the church. Have you been interested enough in this to favor one side over the other? (If yes) Which do you think: schools should be allowed to start each day with a prayer or religion does not belong in the schools?"

23. This point is often obscured because of subsequent events in the Vietnam War. In a manner not dissimilar to Social Security and government owned electric power plants, the Democrats exaggerated Goldwater's political position. Having made a disastrous comment about the use of "tactical nuclear weapons" by field commanders, Goldwater was pictured as an advocate of war. See White (1965: 309-316). The subsequent escalation of the "Vietnam conflict" into the "War in Southeast Asia" portrayed Lyndon Johnson as a war President, thus obscuring the difference between the two candidates in 1964. Nevertheless, it is a major assumption of this research that the alternatives on *domestic* issues presented to the electorate in 1968 were very different.

24. The gamma coefficient is an ordinal measure of association which has a value from −1.00 to +1.00. The statistic may be thought of as the number of agreements in two rank orderings less the number of disagreements expressed as a percentage of the total number of comparisons. For a complete explanation, see L. A. Goodman and W. H. Kruskal (1954: 732-764).

25. On the former influence, see Philip E. Converse (1964: 206-261). On the latter influence, see Donald E. Stokes (1966: 19-28).

26. For a more complete discussion of the various definitions of "ideology," see Broh (1972: Chapter 1).

27. The methodology involved in making this prediction is described in detail in C. Anthony Broh (1972: 41-45). The methodology is based upon an earlier discussion by Charles F. Cnudde (1970: 7-13). See a similar discussion in Hubert M. Blalock (1969: 156-158).

28. Each level of conceptualization of politics reflects the number of likes and dislikes that the respondent volunteered in an open-ended question and that represented a consistent partisan direction. Categories were collapsed as follows: level 1 was a net score of 0 partisanship; level 2 was a net score of −1 or +1; level 3 was −3, −2, +2, +3; level 4 was less than −3 or greater than +3.

29. There is once again a high correlation at the second level of conceptualization suggesting measurement error.

30. Later analysis will show there is some systematic error associated with another control variable.

31. Actually the term "misperception" is a misnomer since it includes non-perceivers. However, the dichotomy is scored the same in a similar variable described by Gerald Pomper (1971; 1972). This scoring is unlike that proposed by Lewis A. Froman, Jr. and James K. Skipper, Jr. (1962), which scored perception accuracy on a four-point scale.

32. Two issues are not shown in Figure 2. At the highest level of conceptualiza-

tion of politics, there was an unexplained increase in gamma correlations; however, the first three levels remain fairly constant. The correlations for Medicare are .02, −.07, .16, .36; and for Equal Job Opportunity are .09, .04, −.05, and .32.

33. One issue has been deleted from Figure 3. The correlations for Equal Job Opportunity were .66, .52, .65, and .78. Again monotonacity is violated at the second level conceptualization of politics.

34. By the time of the 1972 campaign the Democratic Party and the Republican Party had indeed differed in their platforms as suggested on this issue.

35. The three issues are Government Power, Equal Public Accommodations, and Medicare.

36. It is not possible to determine the amount of variance explained from a gamma coefficient. However, by definition the higher the correlation the more variance explained.

37. One such universal proposition might be "all men are mortal" (Blalock, 1969: 11).

38. Of course the only empirical test for this statement is whether the indicator correlates as expected with other known variables. See Kerlinger (1964: 444-462). A brief discussion of measurement can be found in Hubert M. Blalock, Jr. (1960: 8-11).

39. On the relationship of causal language to mathematical language, see Hubert M. Blalock, Jr. (1961: 27-30).

40. An interesting discussion of science viewing "theory" as, what scholars of a discipline say it is, can be found in Thomas S. Kuhn (1962). Much the same impression is gained from Claire Selltiz, Marie Jahoda, Morton Deutsch, and Stuart W. Cook (1951).

41. Some sociologists who have written about the declining importance of ideology in American society are, Daniel Bell (1960), Seymour Martin Lipset (1959), and David Riesman (1961).

REFERENCES

BELL, DANIEL (1960) The End of Ideology. Glencoe, Ill.: Free Press.

BERELSON, BERNARD R., PAUL F. LAZARSFELD, and WILLIAM N. McPHEE (1954) Voting: A Study of Opinion Formation in a Presidential Campaign. Chicago: Univ. of Chicago Press.

BLALOCK, HUBERT M., Jr. (1961) Causal Inferences in Nonexperimental Research. Chapel Hill: Univ. of North Carolina Press.

--- (1960) Social Statistics. New York: McGraw-Hill.

--- (1969) Theory Construction: From Verbal to Mathematical Formulations. Englewood Cliffs, N.J.: Prentice-Hall.

BOYD, RICHARD W. (1972) "Popular control of public policy: a normal vote analysis of the 1968 election." Amer. Pol. Sci. Rev. (June): 429-449.

BROH, C. ANTHONY (1972) "Issue attitudes, conceptualization, and perception: toward a theory of issue voting." Ph.D. dissertation, University of Wisconsin. (unpublished)

CAMPBELL, ANGUS (1966) "Book reviews." Amer. Pol. Sci. Rev. (December): 1007-1008.

——— PHILLIP E. CONVERSE, WARREN E. MILLER, and DONALD E. STOKES (1966) Elections and the Political Order. New York: John Wiley.

——— (1960) The American Voter. New York: John Wiley.

CNUDDE, CHARLES F. (1970) "Theories of political development and the assumptions of statistical models: an evaluation of two models." Paper presented at the 66th meeting of the American Political Science Association, Los Angeles, California.

CONVERSE, PHILIP E. (1964) "The nature of belief systems in mass publics," pp. 206-261 in D. Apter (ed.), Ideology and Discontent. Glencoe, Ill.: Free Press.

DOWNS, ANTHONY (1957) An Economic Theory of Democracy. New York: Harper and Row.

FIELD, JOHN OSGOOD and RONALD E. ANDERSON (1969) "Ideology in the public's conceptualization of the 1964 election." Public Opinion Q. (Fall): 380-398.

FROMAN, LEWIS A., Jr., and JAMES K. SKIPPER, Jr. (1962) "Factors related to misperceiving party stands on issues." Public Opinion Q.: 265-272.

GOLDWATER, BARRY M. (1960) The Conscience of a Conservative. New York: MacFadden.

GOODMAN, L. A. and W. H. KRUSKAL (1954) "Measures of association for cross classification." J. of the Amer. Statistical Assn.: 732-764.

JOHNSON, LYNDON BAINES (1971) The Vantage Point: Perspectives of the Presidency 1963-1969. New York: Holt, Rinehart & Winston.

KERLINGER, FRED N. (1964) Foundations of Behavioral Research: Education and Psychological Inquiry. New York: Holt, Rinehart & Winston.

KESSEL, JOHN H. (1972) "Comment: the issues in issue voting." Amer. Pol. Sci. Rev. (June): 459-465.

——— (1968) The Goldwater Coalition: Republican Strategies in 1964. Indianapolis: Bobbs-Merrill.

KEY, V. O., Jr. (1966) The Responsible Electorate: Rationality in Presidential Voting 1936-1960. New York: Vintage.

KUHN, THOMAS S. (1962) The Structure of Scientific Revolutions. Chicago: Univ. of Chicago Press.

LEEGE, DAVID C. (1972) "Communications." Amer. Pol. Sci. Rev. (September): 1008-1009.

LIPSET, SEYMOUR MARTIN (1959) Political Man: The Social Bases of Politics. Garden City: Doubleday Anchor.

MEEHAN, EUGENE, J. (1967) Contemporary Political Thought: A Critical Study. Homewood, Ill.: Dorsey.

MINAR, DAVID W. (1961) "Ideology and political behavior." Midwest J. of Pol. Sci. (November): 317-331.

PAGE, BENJAMIN I. and RICHARD A. BRODY (1972) "Policy voting and the electoral process: the Vietnam war issue." Amer. Pol. Sci. Rev. (September): 979-995.

PIERCE, JOHN C. (1970) "Party identification and the changing role of ideology in American politics." Midwest J. of Pol. Sci. (February): 25-42.

POMPER, GERALD M. (1972) "From confusion to clarity: issues and American voters, 1956-1968." Amer. Pol. Sci. Rev. (June): 415-428.

——— (1971) "Toward a more responsible two-party system? What, again?" J. of Politics (November): 916-940.

RePASS, DAVID E. (1971) "Issue salience and party choice." Amer. Pol. Sci. Rev. (June): 389-400.

RIESMAN, DAVID (1961) The Lonely Crowd: A Study of the Changing American Character. New Haven: Yale Univ. Press.

SELLTIZ, CLAIR, MARIE JAHODA, MORTON DEUTSCH and STUART W. COOK (1951) Research Methods in Social Relations. New York: Holt, Rinehart & Winston.

STOKES, DONALD E. (1966) "Some dynamic elements of contests for the presidency." Amer. Pol. Sci. Rev. (March): 19-28.

WASBY, STEPHEN L. (1970) The Impact of the United States Supreme Court: Some Perspectives. Homewood, Ill.: Dorsey.

WEISBERG, HERBERT and JERROLD G. RUSK (1970) "Dimensions of candidate evaluation." Amer. Pol. Sci. Rev. (December): 1167-1185.

WHITE, THEODORE H. (1965) The Making of the President 1964. New York: Atheneum.

C. ANTHONY BROH is Assistant Professor of Political Science at the State University of New York at Geneseo. He received his Ph.D. from the University of Wisconsin. His areas of interest include survey research, voting behavior and political parties—with special reference to American government and politics.